Illinois Native Americans

A Kid's Look at Our State's Chiefs, Tribes, Reservations, Powwows, Lore, and More From The Past and the Present

By Carole Marsh

Native American Heritage™

Graphic Design: Lynette Rowe • Cover Design: Victoria DeJoy

NATIVE AMERICAN HERITAGE™

CAROLE MARSH BOOKS

Published by
GALLOPADE™ INTERNATIONAL
800-536-2GET
www.gallopade.com

Gallopade is proud to be a member of these educational organizations and associations:

The National School Supply and Equipment Association (NSSEA)
American Booksellers Association (ABA)
Virginia Educational Media Association (VEMA)
Association of Partners for Public Lands (APPL)
Museum Store Association (MSA)
National Association for Gifted Children (NAGC)
Publishers Marketing Association (PMA)
International Reading Association (IRA)
Association of African American Museums (AAAM)

Native American Heritage™ Series

Native American
Big Activity Book

Native American
Biographies

Native American
Coloring Book

Native American
Heritage Book

Native American
Timeline

Illinois State Stuff™

- My First Pocket Guide: Illinois
- My First Book About Illinois
- Illinois Coloring Book
- The Big Illinois Reproducible Activity Book
- Jeopardy: Answers & Questions About Our State
- Illinois "Jography!": A Fun Run Through Our State
- Illinois Gamebooks
- Illinois Bingo Games
- Illinois Illustrated Timelines
- Illinois Project Books
- Illinois Bulletin Board Set
- Illinois PosterMap
- Illinois Stickers
- Let's Discover Illinois! CD-ROM

Word from the Author

Hello!

I hope you are as interested in North America's wonderful Indian heritage as I am!

Like most kids, I grew up thinking of Indians as the other half of Cowboys. Today, of course, we are getting a much clearer and more accurate picture of what the first peoples on our land were all about. These "facts" are much more fascinating than anything Hollywood can make up. And you probably won't find much of this information in your history textbook!

I am 1/16 Cherokee. This is something I am very proud of and happy about. My grandmother was 1/4 Cherokee. She had tan skin, long gray hair and a very Indian look – especially if I did something bad! Her maiden name was Carrie Corn. Of course, when she got married, she took her husband's name, so it was many years before I learned to appreciate the significance of my native heritage.

Today, I'm trying to make up for lost time by exploring my roots as deeply as I can. One of the most interesting things I've learned is how fascinating all of the Indian tribes are – in the past, the present and future!

As you read about "your" Indians, remember that all native peoples were part of an ever-changing network of time, ideas, power and luck — good and bad. This is certainly a history that is not "dead," but continues to change – often right outside our own back doors! – all the time.

Carole Marsh
She-Who-Writes

PS: Many references show different spellings for the same word. I have tried to select the most common spelling for the time period described. I would not want to be in an Indian spelling bee!

A is for . . .

Alton, Illinois

Site of an Indian pictograph of a thunderbird, seen by explorers in 1673, but was quarried away in 1867.

Awl

An Indian's "needle." Often made from wood, thorns, bone, or metal, it was used to punch holes in skins so they could be sewn together.

Adze

An Indian woodworking tool used to cut, scrape, or gouge; often used to hollow dugout canoes. Blades were made of stone, shell, bone or copper.

American Indian Library Association

Chicago; helps develop and improve libraries on Indian reservations and at other Native American populated sites.

Albany Mounds

Near Princeton. One of the largest Hopewell Indian sites in Illinois; contains at least 90 mounds.

Altar

A platform made of rocks or animal skulls; some had bowls, feathers, rattles, or skins on them. Indians prayed at these altars for things like good crops or expert hunting skills.

Arrow

A long, slender shaft made of reed, cane, or wood; pointed tip was attached to one end and split feathers to the other. Feathers helped the arrows fly straight.

Arts and Crafts

Early Illinois Indians made beautifully decorated pottery, finely carved stone figures of animals and human beings and sparkling jewelry.

Aborigine

A member of the earliest known population of a region.

Arrowhead

The pointed tip of an arrow, made of bone, antler, wood, or iron. Some tips had barbs that would embed themselves in flesh. These barbs made it difficult for an enemy to remove the arrowhead from a wound.

B is for . . .

Black Hawk

Famous chief of the Sac (Sauk) and Fox Indians. Born in 1767 in Illinois. Became a warrior at age 15. Fought with the English during the War of 1812. Defeated during the Black Hawk War. Was dressed in a uniform General Andrew Jackson had given him and buried Indian style — above ground! His bones were sent to Quincy, Illinois and made into a skeleton.

Band

A subdivision of an Indian tribe. In earlier times, a band was sometimes created when part of a tribe split off from the main group. The band also chose new leadership.

Blankets

Used for door covers, partitions, bags, to dry food on, carry babies and many other purposes.

Black Partridge

Potawatomi chief who warned the whites at Fort Dearborn that they might be attacked if they left the fort, but they did so against his advice.

Black Hawk War

In 1829, while his tribe was on their winter hunt, white squatters moved into Black Hawk's village. The Indians returned, and lived side by side with the squatters who would not leave. When the Indians returned from their winter hunt again the next spring, government officials decided to evict the Indians, and started Black Hawk's War. It was an ugly war—both sides engaged in brutal acts. In the end, Black Hawk escaped and his warriors were trapped and massacred.

Black Hawk Statue

Stands on the Rock River at Oregon, Illinois. With folded arms, he majestically stands guard over the lands he once ruled!

Bow

Made from wood, horn or bone. Illinois Indian children learned how to use bows. The bowstring was made from animal gut, rawhide or twisted vegetable fibers.

Bone

Animal bones were used by Illinois Indians to make buttons, whistles and other items.

Beads

Made of wood, shells, claws, minerals, seeds — you name it! Later, the Illinois Indians traded with white men for glass beads, used in some of their decorative arts.

C is for . . .

Chief

Leader of a tribe. Different titles meant different things. Some members were made chief because they owned deeds to land. Chieftainship was often inherited, usually from the mother!

Checagou

A swampy area of land on the shore of Lake Michigan that the Indians were forced to give up. Name comes from the wild onions that once grew in the marshlands here.

Contact Period

What historians call the era in the 1500s when Native Americans first met Europeans. This meeting changed the lifestyle of the Illinois Indians more than anyone could ever have anticipated!

Chicago

Has long been one of the U.S. sites for an Indian relocation office, which helps Native Americans leaving reservations to find jobs in cities. Also, the name of an Illinois Indian chief and a site on Lake Michigan called "the place of the skunk" because such an animal was killed here by the Fox Indians.

Chert

A type of flint found in Illinois. Is light in color and was used by the Indians to make tools, knives, arrow and spearheads.

Caddo

Indian tribe that pierced their noses, tattooed themselves and traded horses as far north as Illinois.

Clan

A tribal unit. Members are descended from the same ancestor.

Cahokia Mounds

Near Collinsville. Site of a city inhabited from A.D. 850 to 1500 by prehistoric Indians. Around 65 earthen ceremonial and burial mounds are preserved here. A historic site and museum include artifacts, a stockade, garden, wall trench house and more.

Chicago Treaty

In 1833, many Indian lands were ceded to the U.S. Government under this treaty. After this, many Indians that once lived in Illinois moved west.

Cahokia

A band of the Illinois Indians.

D is for . . .

Dearborn

Site of a fort where the Chicago River flowed into Lake Michigan. During the War of 1812, the British got the Indians to attack American frontier settlements. Fearful of such a siege, the people here were ordered to go to Fort Wayne in Indiana for safety. As they made their way south, they were attacked by 400 Potawatomi warriors. Even though the children threw rocks, and wives wrestled in hand-to-hand struggles and the men fought with rifles, swords and tomahawks, they were defeated in only 15 minutes!

Dance

There were Indian dances for every occasion: war, peace, hunting, rain, good harvests, etc. Drums, rattles, and flutes of bone or reed provided the music. Dancers often chanted or sang while performing. Steps were not easy to learn and required consistent practice.

Disease

Illinois Indians had no immunity to the diseases that white explorers, colonists and settlers brought to their lands. These diseases included smallpox, measles, tuberculosis and others, which ravaged the tribes in great epidemics that killed many, and sometimes all, members of a tribe.

Dr. Carlos Montezuma

Apache named Wasajah, who as a boy, was sold to a prospector for $30. He brought the boy to Chicago and gave him his new name. He attended the Chicago public schools and the University of Illinois. He was graduated from the Chicago Medical School and practiced medicine in Chicago and on Indian reservations. He also taught and wrote.

Dickson Mounds

Lewiston; Mississippian and Middle Woodlands sites located here; there's also a museum of archaeological exhibits, including skeletons, tools and weapons, just as they were buried by the Indians.

Delaware Indians

Tribe also called the Lenni Lenape; came to Illinois to flee the domination of the Iroquois—the most important Algonquian confederacy. The English called them Delawares from their river. The French called them loups or "wolves."

Dramatic Hair!

The Sac (Sauk) and Fox tribes were known for their big tuft of deer hair dyed red worn atop their head, which they had shaven bare!

Dreams

Important in the Indian tradition. It was believed that dreams were the "windows" to the soul. Many thought a person's hidden desires were expressed in dreams.

E is for . . .

Eagle

An animal used in many Indian ceremonies. Eagle feathers attached to war bonnets and shields communicated an Indian's rank in his tribe and what kinds of deeds he had done. Feathers also adorned rattles, pipes, baskets, and prayer sticks.

Effigy Mound Culture

Built earthen figures of birds, animals or people.

Emmegahbowh

Methodist Indian minister born into the Ottawa tribe and adopted by the Chippewa as a boy. Attended the Missionary School in Jacksonville, Illinois. When ordained as a minister, was given the name Rev. John Johnson.

Early Artisans

Ancient Great Lakes artisans learned how to hammer copper into axheads and spear points. They often found copper lying in chunks on the ground. By trial and error, they learned how to remove raw copper from inside certain rocks.

Earrings

Medicine men sometimes pierced male and female ears at special ceremonies. Earrings, which cost parents or relatives a significant amount, symbolized wealth and distinction. The more earrings that an Indian wore, the greater his honor. Some earrings measured 12 inches in length!

Environment

Preserving the environment is important to preserving Native American heritage. For thousands of years, Native American tribes lived completely off the land. Farming, mining, pollution have all had a part in changing native environments.

English

In the 1800s, the U.S. government built boarding schools for Indian children throughout the nation. Children were forced to leave their homes and families to live at these schools. They were required to learn English and not speak their native languages.

Epidemics

Few Indians possessed immunity to the deadly diseases, like smallpox and measles, which European explorers and settlers brought to the New World. As a result, great population loss took place. Sometimes entire tribes became extinct. Epidemics sparked by Hernando De Soto's expedition are estimated to have killed 75% of the native population in the New World.

F is for . . .

Fetish

These small objects were thought to hold the spirit of an animal or a part of nature. A fetish could be an object found in nature, such as bone or wood, or it could be a carved object. The fetish was usually small enough to be carried in a small bag or on a cord. The making and use of a fetish was kept secret by its owner and only shared with the one who inherited it.

Fox

The native name for the tribe is "Mesquaki", meaning "red earth people". They were seminomadic. Raised crops in the summer, but hunted on the trail in the winter. Had three kinds of leaders—the peace chief, the war chief, and the ceremonial leader. Formed an alliance with the Sac (Sauk) in 1734 that continues today.

Fort Massac

On the Ohio River; built by French soldiers as a stronghold against Indians, but only one skirmish ever occurred here — with the Cherokee.

Fire Drill

A device used by Indians to make fires which consisted of a stick and a piece of wood with a tight hole in it. The stick was twirled rapidly in the hole, creating friction that would ignite shredded grass or wood powder placed nearby to start a fire.

French and Indian War

Broke out in 1745 over boundary lines between New France and the British colonies. The British defeated the French and their Indian allies. A peace treaty in 1763 ended the war, when Canada and most French possessions east of the Mississippi River were given to the English.

Fort St. Louis

One of the chain of forts built to try to strengthen the relationship between the French and more than 18,000 Illini Confederation Indians who sought refuge from Iroquois raids.

Footwear

Illinois Indians wore different footwear depending on their tribe and environment. Moccasins were made mostly of animal skin. Sandals were made of rawhide or plant material.

Fur Trade

Begun when the Europeans came eager to grow rich from the pelts of animals. Trading had a powerful impact on the Indian. To get the newcomers' goods, Indians worked as trappers for the French. A flintlock gun cost 12 beaver pelts. But the ultimate cost was much more expensive — the loss of the Indian's way of life. Many Indians abandoned their traditional farming for trapping and came to depend on the Europeans.

G is for . . .

Games

Adults played ball and other games of chance or skill. Indian children spun tops, fought pretend battles, did target-shooting, walked on stilts, played hide and seek, or competed to see who could hold their breath the longest!

Golden Garbage!

Illinois archaeologists have uncovered ancient garbage heaps made of animal bones and big piles of clam shells in Illinois. This trash full of treasures has helped them understand the early native inhabitants of our state better.

Grand Medicine Society

Also called the Midewiwin Society. This was an exclusive club with elaborate rituals that were important in tribal and religious matters. One of the tribes with this society was the Potawatomi.

Gens

Group of related members from different tribes.

Gathering

Native Americans gathered natural materials for food, fuel, baskets, clothing, and housing. American Indians tribes also hunted to meet basic needs. Even though some tribes planted crops, most did some kind of gathering.

Gorgets

Beautiful ornaments hung around the neck or from ears; their significance, if any, is unknown.

Gourds

Hollowed-out shell of a gourd plant's dried fruit which often grew into a specific shape. Indians raised many species of gourds. They were used for spoons, bowls, masks, rattles, and even storage.

Go To These Exciting Illinois Indian Events!

Annual Potawatomi Trail Pow wow – May, Taylorville; Annual Return to Pimiteoui Powwow – June, Peoria; Annual New Windsor Pow Wow – June, New Windsor; Potawatomi Trails Traditional/Social Pow-Wow – August, Shiloh Park Zion; Annual Chicago American Indian Center Powwow – November, Chicago.

H is for . . .

Hatchet

A small, short-handled ax, primarily used as a tool, not as a weapon. When settlers moved in, stone hatchets were replaced with iron ones.

Hair

Indians used hair as a textile. Hair from bison, mountain sheep, elk, moose, deer, dog, rabbit, beaver, or even humans were used to weave cloth, make wigs, or stuff pillows, balls, dolls or drumsticks.

Horn and Hooves

Indians used animal horn to make spoons and dishes. Hooves were made into rattles and bird beaks were used for decoration.

Hopewell Culture

Early people who lived in the Ohio Valley from about 100 B.C. to A.D. 500. Anthropologists believe they had a layered society with a defined organization and code of conduct. Because of this, they could work together to build great earthenworks called mounds. They also had an extensive trade network from the Midwest to the eastern U.S. seacoast.

Hauberg Indian Museum

Rock Island. Depicts the life of the Sac (Sauk) and Mesquakie Indians during the period when they were trying to save their lands.

Hunters

Early Indian peoples were hunters who used wooden spears with stone points to kill many kinds of large mammals that are extinct today, such as mammoths and mastodons!

Horses

Spaniards brought the horse to America. At first, Indians were afraid of the horse. Later, Indians "broke" horses gently, often "hypnotizing" them with a blanket. Horses were used for transportation, trade, barter or payment.

Huron

Powerful traders who lived on the Canada side of the Great Lakes. Iroquois invasions scattered the Huron and caused a series on migrations to the U.S. side of the lakes in the late 1600s, into the 1700s. By 1842 they had sold their lands and were moved to Indian Territory. Their native name, Wyandot, used when talking about tribal members who relocated to the U.S.

Historic Site

Near Rock Island; 207 acres of rugged woodlands once occupied by the Sac (Sauk) and Mesquakie Indian tribes.

I is for . . .

Illinois Indians

Confederacy of Algonquian tribes that lived in Illinois. Their name was a combination of Indian and French. Algonquian "illini" meant "man." It was an Illinois that killed Chief Pontiac in 1769, which caused many tribes to make war on them and almost wipe them out.

Illinois

The state and river named for the shortened term of the Illiniwek Territory.

Indian Removal Act of 1830

This federal act gave President Andrew Jackson the power to relocate tribes east of the Mississippi to an "Indian Territory." The forced removal of the southeast Indians later became known as the "Trail of Tears."

Illiniwek

The people who gave their name to the state of Illinois. Lived here after the Mississippi culture had died out. Their name meant "the men" or "the superior men." They were a confederation of several groups of Indians who spoke Algonquian languages. Lived mainly on rivers and streams. Built long, narrow houses with birch frames covered by mats of woven grass and mud. Lived from the fertile plains, by either hunting game, catching fish or growing corn, squash and pumpkins.

Independence

Native American tribes are sovereign nations. That means they are independent. Some even issue their own passports! However, Native Americans are also considered citizens of the United States and enjoy all the rights and privileges of U.S. citizens.

Indian Ladder

Indians made ladders by trimming branches off a tree. Some were left at consistent intervals to provide steps.

Indian Tribes in Illinois

At one time or another, these tribes have lived in the state of Illinois:

Fox, Huron (Wyandot), Illinois, Kickapoo, Miami, Potawatomi, Sac, Shawnee

Indian

In 1493, Christopher Columbus called the native people he met in North America "Indians" because he mistakenly believed he had sailed to India! Today, this term includes the aborigines of North and South America.

J is for . . .

Just So You Know . . .

Today you can find many Illinois Indians that follow some traditional ways. But there are also many who are entrepreneurs, doctors, lawyers, educators and even politicians! If you visit a reservation or cultural event, make sure you know visitor etiquette. Often dances are religious ceremonies and should be observed as such; religious dances should not be applauded. Photography, videotaping and drawing are all important issues - check with the tribe or individual before any is started.

Jesuits

Roman Catholic priests called Jesuits were among the first to meet and live with the North American Indians. Their writings, sent back to Europe, serve as one of today's best references to early Indian life.

Justice?

For hundreds of years, Native Americans have not received justice from federal and state governments. Native Americans have had nearly all their land taken away. Native Americans still have to fight for their rights in courts across the land.

Judicial Termination

Modern term to describe current efforts by various U.S. government agencies and officials (especially the judicial system) to legally decrease the sovereignty of independent Indian tribes.

Just In Time!

The Indian Arts and Crafts Act of 1990 makes it against the law to pretend that an item has been made by Native Americans if it is really not. It is illegal to offer or display for sale, or sell any art or craft product in a way that falsely suggests it is Indian produced.

Jerked Meat

Thin strips of buffalo, elk, deer or other animal meat which is dried on racks in the sun; also called "jerky."

K is for . . .

Keokuk

Sac (Sauk) leader born in 1780 in Illinois. As a "guest keeper," he would entertain people at tribal expense. This gave him great influence and power, so much so, that he was made a chief after the Black Hawk War.

Kickapoo

Algonquian Indian tribe that migrated to Illinois in the 1760s and stayed until the 1830s Allied with the Sac (Sauk) and Fox from early history. Some fought in the Black Hawk War of 1832. Name of an Illinois creek.

Killed Pottery

Pottery placed in a grave as an offering to the dead person was called killed pottery. A hole was formed in its base during creation. Often broken pottery was placed in a grave because Indians believed the spirit of the dead person would then be released and could travel.

Kilatika

Division of the Miami Indian tribe that lived in upper Illinois in 1684.

Kaskaskia

Town in Randolph County on the Kaskaskia River. Believed to be the oldest town in the Mississippi Valley. The name comes from the Indian tribe that once lived here. Means "he scrapes it off with a tool." Was founded by the French and served as the capital of the Illinois Territory until Illinois became a state in 1818.

Kanakuk

Kickapoo Indian chief who lived in Illinois and died of smallpox in 1852.

L is for . . .

Linguistic Families

There are 56 related groups of American Indian languages. A few of these speech families include Iroquoian, Algonquian, Siouan, Muskogean, Athapascan, and Wakashan.

Leggings

Both men and women wore cloth or skin covering, which were often decorated with quills, beads, or painted designs, for their legs.

Lost Tribes of Israel

This historic theory has been floating around since 721 BC. The 10 lost tribes of Israel are supposedly groups of people gathered together by Sargon, the King of Assyria. Some say he cast out 10 of the 12 tribes of Israel. Many have tried to prove that the American Indians are these missing tribes!

Lenni Lenape

Also called the Delaware Indians; originally from that state. Forced to give up lands many times. Lived in at least 10 different states and signed 45 different treaties, often believing they were leasing the land. They sold Manhattan island, signed the Penn treaties, and were the first tribe to sign a treaty with the U.S.!

Lodge

The term for a type of Indian house that was usually a permanent dwelling. The population of a tribe was often estimated by its number of lodges.

Land Loss

Native Americans lost their land in many ways. Conflicts with other tribes, colonization, European settlement, treaties, and removal took away Indian lands.

Lariat

These throw ropes made of rawhide, buffalo hair, or horsehair sometimes measured up to 20 feet long!

Lance

Spear used for hunting and war. The hunting lance had a short shaft and a broad, heavy head. The war lance was light and had a long shaft.

Larsen Site

At Dickson Mounds. Site where early Illinois Indians lived in fortified villages, where farming was their chief activity.

M is for . . .

Miami

Algonquian Indian tribe who formed a crucial alliance with the Shawnee. They called themselves Twightwees, a name that came from the cry of the crane. Worshiped the sun and thunder. Lived in houses covered with bark or rush mats.

Maize

Also called Indian Corn. Known as a "cereal" plant because it probably began as some form of grass. The Indians in our state figured out every possible way to use corn as a food. The only thing the white man added was the creation of "corn flakes!"

Monk's Mound

Cahokia, near East St. Louis. Center of worship for a city that may have had 100,000 people at one time! Largest earthwork in the world!!

Mounds

Great hills of earth made by human hands. Can be round with broad, flat tops, cone-shaped, or in the shape of animals. Created by early peoples of Illinois. Were used to mark graves of important community members. Around 10,000 Indian mounds have been found in Illinois!

Minemaung

Potawatomi village located in Kankakee County. Was ceded to the U.S. by a treaty in 1832.

Messipi

What the Indians called today's Mississippi River. The name meant "Father of All Waters."

Mound Builders

About 2,000 years ago a wave of migrating people came to our area. They were the first of many groups to be known as the Mound Builders, for the earthenworks they created. Sometimes built high earthen walls around their villages, possibly for defense. They vanished long before the first white explorers reached Illinois.

N is for . . .

Nomadic

A way of life in which people frequently moved from one location to another in search of food. "Seminomadic" people had permanent villages, but left them in certain seasons to hunt, fish, or gather wild plant foods.

Natural History Museum

University of Illinois, Urbana; prehistoric and historic collections, with a special focus on Illinois Indians.

Nation

There are many Indian nations located within the United States, such as the Potawatomi Nation. Indian nations are called nations because their governments and laws are independent of and separate from the U.S. government. The federal government must have "government to government" relations with these Indian nations, just as it would with foreign nations, like England or Spain.

November

In 1990, President George Bush approved a joint resolution designating November 1990 "National American Indian Heritage Month." Similar proclamations have been issued each year since 1994.

Names

Indian names were often changed during one's lifetime. These names could be derived from events that happened during the person's birth, childhood, adolescence, war service, or retirement from active tribal life. Some names came from dreams, some were inherited, and sometimes names were stolen or taken in revenge. Today some Indians maintain old, traditional Indian names, while others take modern names. Since settlers often did not read or write Indian languages, they recorded Indian names phonetically (as they "sounded"). Thus Indian names were often misspelled.

National Museum of the American Indian

The Smithsonian's National Museum of the American Indian on the National Mall in Washington, D.C., symbolizes a deeper understanding between America's first citizens and those who have come to make these shores their home.

Native American Educational Services College

Tribal Research Center, Chicago; programs and degrees available in Indian studies of all types; courses may be taken at various sites in the state.

O is for . . .

Old Bones

No one knows for sure when the first people came to North America, but scientists have dated bones and artifacts discovered at Clovis, New Mexico around 11,200 years old. Testing on a skeleton found on the Channel Islands, off the coast of California showed they were about 13,000 years old. And, evidence of human habitation in southern New Mexico suggests that people may have been there as far back as 38,000 years ago.

Osage

Indian tribe that once lived along thee Ohio River valley before migrating to the eastern plains.

Origins

Some scientists believe that Native Americans actually came across a land bridge between Asia and North America. They say that during an ice age thousands of years ago, the water level was much lower and people could have walked between the two continents.

Ogden-Fettie Site

At Dickson Mounds. Small settlement where Indians sustained themselves by hunting and gathering.

Oil

Indians extracted oil from the many layers of fat that came with fresh bear meat. The fat was boiled down in earthen pots to produce the oil, which was stored in gourds and pots. The oil was used for cooking and even beautifying the body! Indians would mix red pigment with the oil, add the fragrances of cinnamon and sassafras, and rub it all over their bodies.

Orators

Many Indian leaders were excellent public speakers. Powerful and dramatic speakers were vital to leaders who wanted to influence their tribe. Watch for famous Indian quotations in literature and textbooks!

Office of Indian Education Programs

This is a service organization devoted to providing quality education opportunities for American Indian people. Established in the latter part of the nineteenth century to carry out the federal government's education commitment to Indian tribes, it has become the only national education system for American Indian children and adults.

P is for . . .

Potawatomi

Part of the Council of Three Fires. Burned away grass and brush to clear fields for planting. Principal crops were corn, beans, squash and tobacco. After the harvest, they moved their villages into the forests to be protected from the winter winds. Once lived where Chicago now stands. Played a major role in the Ft. Dearborn massacre.

Piasa

Name of the thunderbird and a pictograph seen on rocks near Alton, Illinois around 1673. Name means "bird that eats men."

Peoria

Former Illinois Indian tribe that lived along the Mississippi River. Name means "he comes carrying a pack on his back." The name came from an Illinois chief.

Paint

Indians used many natural materials to make paint, like clay mixed with oil or grease. Yellow "paint" was made with the gall bladder of a buffalo! Why did they paint their faces or bodies? Indians used paint to look scary or beautiful, to disguise themselves, or to protect their skin from sunburn or insect bites. Indians often applied red paint because it symbolized strength and success. That is why settlers often referred to the Indians as Red Men.

Pecan

Sometimes called the "Illinois nut;" was much prized by Indians.

Pemmican

Indian food made of animal meat, which was dried in the sun, pounded together with fat and berries. The mixture was packed into skin bags and used primarily while on the trail.

Pokagon, Simon

Chief of the Pokagon band of the Potawatomi Indians. His father once owned the land where Chicago stands now. Born in 1830. At the age of 14, was sent to school. Spoke many languages and was probably the most educated Indian of his day. Wrote many magazine articles and a book, printed on birch bark. Managed tribal affairs for 43 years, even helping collect a $150,000 claim from the Government. Died in 1899.

Parker, General Eli Samuel

Part Seneca; grandson of Chief Red Jacket. Worked in Galena, Illinois during the Civil War as an engineer.

Pontiac, Chief

Brilliant Ottawa leader. In 1763, led an uprising of Great Lakes Indians against British rule.

Q is for . . .

Quillwork

Indians used the quills of porcupine or birds to make a type of embroidery. Quills were dyed with juice from berries and other materials. When they were ready to be used, the quills were either mashed with teeth or softened with hot water and flattened with rocks. The quills were then laced into moccasins, shirts, pipe covers, and other items. Beads which Indians received by trading with settlers eventually replaced quillwork.

Quality

Native American arts and crafts are known for their excellent craftsmanship and striking designs. This work is often influenced by things found in nature especially plants and animals.

Quiver

Case used to hold arrows; made of woven plant materials or animal skins.

Quarry Site

A location where Indians went for workable stone such as flint and made stone tools.

Quirt

A short riding whip with a wood, bone, or horn handle.

R is for . . .

Rain Dancing

The rain dance ceremony, performed to encourage rainfall, was common among Indian religions because good weather is vital for a successful harvest. Rainmakers were in tune with nature; there are actual reported cases of Indians producing or preventing rain!

Roots

Indians used plant roots for food, medicine, dye, baskets, cloth, rope, salt, flavoring, and just to chew!

Rattles

Indians of Illinois made rattles from bird beaks, animal hooves, bones, pods, seashells, turtle shells and other animal parts. The rattles are used in ceremonies.

Rock River Country

In northwestern Illinois; once the exclusive territory of the Sac (Sauk) and Fox Indians.

Rawhide

Untanned animal hide. The "green" hide was stretched on the ground or over a frame. Flesh and fat were removed. The skin was dried, washed, then buried with wood ashes which made the hair come off. Used by the Illinois Indian to make drumheads, lash lodge poles, mend broken objects and in many other ways.

Reservations

The U.S. government set aside, or "reserved," land for the Indians. These reservations originally served as a sort of prison during the beginning stages of Indian removal. At that time, reservations provided the government with some control over Indian activity and residency. This land was usually considerably less desirable land than the Indians' native territories. Today's reservations are lands that are tribally held, yet protected by the government.

Removal

The U.S. government policy of the 1830s-1850s that removed Indians from their native lands to new lands, primarily west of the Mississippi River.

S is for . . .

Saukenuk

Capital of the Sac (Sauk) Indian nation and from 1740-1820, one of the largest Indian villages in North America. Site of the westernmost battle of the Revolutionary War, when in 1780, American troops destroyed the village to end the Indian's alliance with the British.

Shobonier

1830 Potawatomi village in De Kalb County, Illinois. Named after a chief. Present site of the town of Shabbona.

Shaman

Medicine man and spiritual leader who was supposed to have special healing power from another world.

Shawnee

Indians who migrated north from Kentucky and North Carolina. They split into different groups and migrated often. Introduced cultural traits of the southern tribes to the northern tribes, and vice versa. Had villages along rivers in Ohio at one time.

Sweatlodge

Structure used for ritual purification by sweating from exposure to very hot fires or hot steam from pouring water over hot stones. Also called a sweathouse, for some tribes also doubling as clubhouses.

Sac (Sauk) and Fox Indian War

Took place in Illinois in 1831.

Sac (Sauk)

Algonquian Woodland Indian tribe that once lived in Illinois.

Shawnee National Forest

Saline springs here were used by prehistoric Indians to get salt.

Shabbona or Shabonee

American appointed Potawatomi "chief." Related to Chief Pontiac. One of Tecumseh's lieutenants. Rode from Princeton, Illinois to Chicago in time to warn people of an Indian attack during the Black Hawk War, which he kept the Potawatomi from joining. Died in Morris, Illinois in 1859 at the age of 84. His grave is in Evergreen Cemetery there.

Stillman Valley

Near Rockford; site of the first skirmish of the Black Hawk War.

Shickshack

Winnebago chief that lived near Salem, Illinois.

T is for . . .

Tobacco

A sacred plant early Indians used to make offering to their gods, cure diseases, bring good luck, seal agreements and bind treaties.

Treaties

Written agreements between the U. S. government and the Indians, most of which involved the Indians giving up their native lands.

Throwing Stick

A sling or grooved stick used to hurl a lance or spear. It was used by Illinois Indians before bows and arrows.

Totem

The spirit of some natural object (usually an animal) taken by an Indian, tribe or family to guard over them.

Tomahawk

A club, axe or hammer used to chop wood, drive stakes in the ground or as a weapon.

Tecumseh

Shawnee leader. Passionate speaker and tireless political organizer. Persuaded the Great Lakes Indians to set aside tribal jealousies and unite against the white enemy.

Tracking

To follow a trail by finding a sign such as a broken blade of grass, a moved stone or moccasin track. Indians learned to trail as children, so that they could find food, track enemies and disguise their own signs.

Teeth

Illinois Indians hung teeth on cords to make necklaces.

Tribe

A group of Indians with shared culture, history, original territory, ancestry, social organization, and governmental structure. A tribe may contain several bands of Indians.

Three Fires

The Potawatomi, Chippewa and Ottawa formed a council by this name. They all spoke Algonquian dialects and shared common cultural traditions, but otherwise had different economies and day-to-day living habits.

Thunderbird

A mythological Indian figure, as well as a part of the constellations for many Indians. Thunderbird mythology is mostly different from tribe to tribe, in general either coexisting with ancestors as an actual bird, or appearing as a spiritual nature god. The Thunderbird was good to the people in either case. Much mythology ties the thunderbird with thunder, lightning and storms.

U is for . . .

U.S. Bureau of Indian Affairs

Provides public services such as law enforcement, land records, economic development, and education to Indians. Known for mismanagement and ethical problems.

U.S. Army

Many Native Americans have fought bravely for the United States Army. Many have also given their lives for a country that was not always accepting of them.

Unique

Each and every tribe has its own unique customs, language, and traditions.

U.S. Indian Schools

The Bureau of Indian Affairs operates hundreds of federal schools around the nation. Enrollment of Native American children measures in the thousands!

U.S. Indian Reorganization Act

Passed by Congress in 1934, the act authorized Indian tribes to establish and conduct their own governments, and to form businesses.

U.S. Colonists

Called Long Knives or Big Knives by early Indians, who also called English explorers "Coat Men."

U.S. Indian Wars

The U.S. War Department has compiled an official list of "Indian Wars" that occurred in the United States. Over 50 wars were fought between the U.S. and the Indians during the period of 1790-1850.

U.S. President

Once called Great White Father by Indians.

V is for . . .

Vessels

Indians carried water in special gourds shaped liked bottles, called water vessels.

Village Councils

These were held in the town (council) house and occurred to discuss and decide important matters. Harmony and agreement was essential to tribal unity. Rather than vote on issues, they were discussed until everyone was satisfied. Anyone who wanted to could speak freely. Everyone did not always agree on the outcome, but everyone avoided conflict by pushing their case.

Vegetable Dyes

Indians could not buy color from the store like we can today. Instead, they created many different colors from the things they found on earth like plants, flowers, shrubs, trees, roots, and berries. They made beautiful and unique reds, oranges, yellows, greens, browns, and violets. These dyes were used for baskets, pottery, weaving, body makeup, and clothing.

Very Hungry

There were Indians who here hunters, gatherers and foragers, that often ate whatever they could find! How hungry would you have to be to eat what they sometimes ate: reptiles, larvae, and insects?

Villages

Many Illinois Indians lived in villages! Villages were formed around different clans or bands within the tribe, but could also contain different clans living together. Villages were usually permanent settlements, although semi-nomadic tribes have been known to migrate between permanent villages.

Vesperic Indians

Indian tribes located in the United States.

W is for . . .

Whirling Thunder

Son of Sauk-Fox chief, Black Hawk. With his father, made an unsuccessful attempt to keep their Illinois homelands.

War Pony

Horse, often painted with colorful paint and ridden into battle.

Woodhenges

Circular sun calendars made of cedar posts found at Cahokia Mounds, largest prehistoric Indian city north of Mexico.

War Dance

Indian braves danced this before going into battle. The dance was a way of assembling the braves and getting them to commit to the fight ahead.

War

The early Illiniwek were in constant war with their Indian neighbors. Intertribal warfare was pretty much a way of life with most North American Indians. But by the mid-1600s, the Iroquois Indians began to invade the fierce Illiniwek territory — and that was a different story!

Wild Rice

A lakeshore crop and one of the chief foods of the Indian of the North Central states, especially the Algonquian tribes of the Great Lakes.

Whistle

Indians from Illinois made them from the wing bones of birds. The whistles made the sound of the bird the bones came from! Used to communicate, signal, sound an alarm or even flirt with a maiden!

War Club

A weapon made of stone, bone, or wood in the shape of a club.

White Man

Indians generally called them Pale Face, a name the white men themselves suggested!

Wabash

Name used by the explorer La Salle in 1682 to mean some of the Indian tribes he met in Illinois. The name means "bright" or "gleaming," referring to the limestone bottom of the Wabash River.

XYZ are for . . .

Xenophobe

A xenophobe is someone who is afraid of foreign people, their customs and cultures, or foreign things. Many of the first European settlers were afraid of Native American cultures.

You Bet!

Some Native Americans say that Casinos make a lot of money. Others say that too many people have a gambling problem. In the 1980s and 1990s, many tribes discussed whether or not gambling casinos should be allowed. Now that many casinos have been built across the country, the debate has switched to how it should be controlled.

Zounds!

Between 1871 and 1913, at least 98 traditional agreements between tribes and the United States were negotiated and 96 of them were ratified by Congress. Each agreement remains as law (unless changed by a later agreement)!

Shamans and medicine men were not the only people who had access to the spirit world. Indians believed that people could make contact with spirits every night in their dreams! Dreamers could travel back to the time of man's creation or far ahead into their own futures. They also believed that dreams contained warnings or commands from the spirits. Many tribes felt that they had to act out their dreams as soon as they awoke. If an Indian dreamed about bathing, for example, he would run to his neighbors' houses first thing in the morning, and his neighbors would throw kettles full of cold water over him.

Y... Or, "Why?"

1. Why do you think Indian warriors carried charms with them? Some Indian medicines have been scientifically proven to have true healing power and are still used today. Do you think their charms had any real power to help them win battles?
2. Why do you think the American government kept relocating Indians onto reservations and then making the reservations smaller and smaller?
3. Why did Indians use items such as a pipe in ceremonies? What kinds of symbolic objects do we use in ceremonies today?
4. Why and how did Indians use natural materials in creative ways?
5. Many Indian tribes are running successful businesses on their reservations today. There is one industry that many tribes are making a lot of money at. Do you know what this is? Hint: "I'll bet you do!"

Which Famous Native American Am I?

Solve the puzzle!

Word Bank

Black Elk	Crazy Horse	Sitting Bull	Sequoia
Sacajawea	Chief Joseph	Geronimo	Pocahontas

Down

1. This Shoshone woman joined Lewis and Clark as their guide and translator and helped make the expedition a success! Hint: She has 4 "a"s in her name!
4. This man gave the Cherokee their first alphabet so that they could write. Until then, they communicated only by speaking and drawing pictures. Hint: A famous ancient tree also has the same name!
5. He was one of the fiercest of Indian warriors! He fought against white settlers in Arizona and New Mexico to keep his people from being pushed off their lands. Hint: Jump!

Across

2. A legend says that this brave Algonquian woman saved the life of Englishman John Smith. Hint: Disney produced a movie about her.
3. He fought at Little Bighorn when he was only 13! He was also a wise "shaman" who saw visions and could advise people. Hint: Part of his name is an animal with antlers!
6. He was a great Sioux warrior who won the battle against General Custer at Little Bighorn in 1876. Hint: His horse was not crazy!
7. A leader of the Lakota (Sioux) tribe who lived on the Standing Rock Reservation in North Dakota after the battle of Little Bighorn. He tried to make conditions better for his people there, so the U.S. government called him a "troublemaker." Hint: He did not sit all the time!
8. A wise and brave chief of the Nez Percé who tried to bring his people to Canada to escape war. He said, "From where the sun now stands, I will fight no more forever." Hint: His father's name was "Old Joseph."

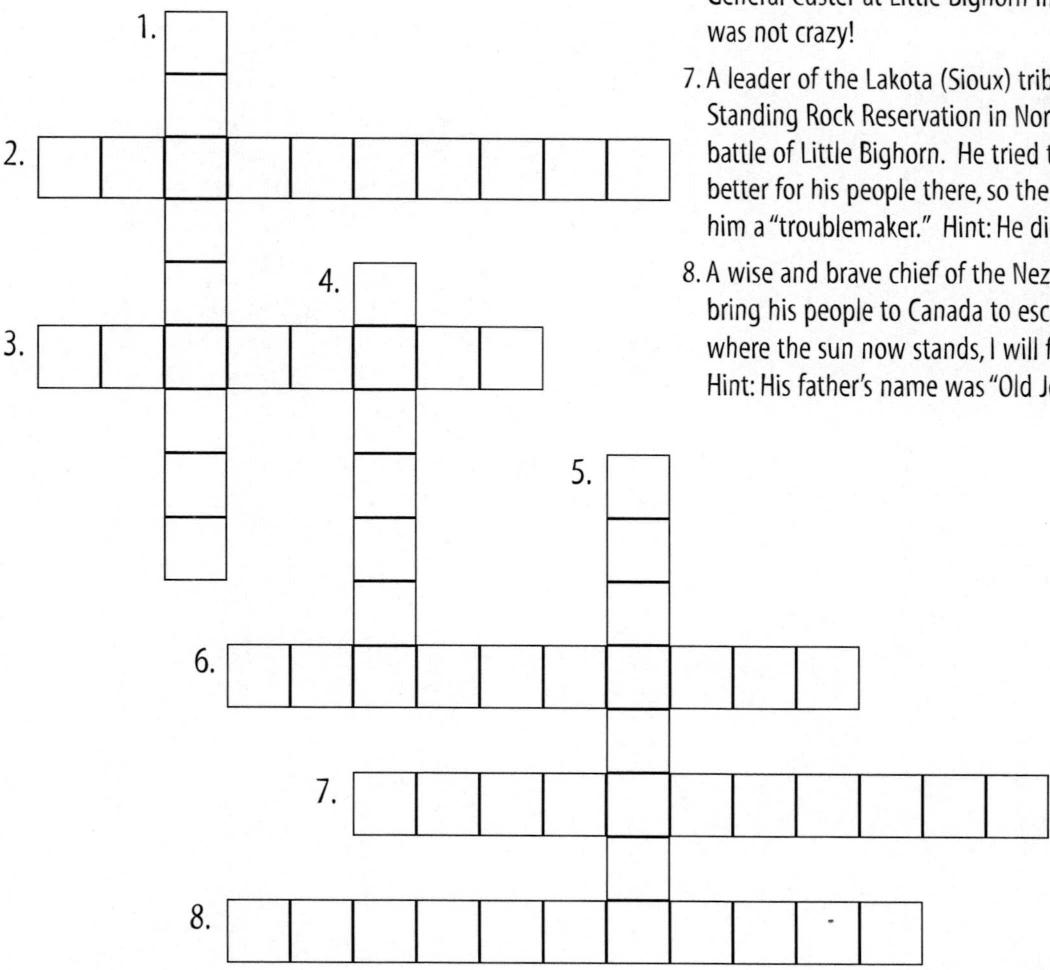

Answer Key: 1. Sacajawea; 2. Pocahontas; 3. Black Elk; 4. Sequoia; 5. Geronimo; 6. Crazy Horse; 7. Sitting Bull; 8. Chief Joseph

Different Ways for Different Indians!

North American Indian tribes are divided into different areas. In each of these areas, tribes shared common ways of living with each other. They might make similar arts or crafts, they might eat the same foods, or they might have had the same beliefs. These activities are all part of their "culture." Each area had its own culture, which was different from the tribes in all the other areas.

Below is a map of all the different groups of Indian tribes in North America. Color each area with a different color. You will see a colorful picture of how Native Americans can all be called "Indians" but still have very different cultures!

Celebration!

Powwows are big festivals where Native Americans gather to sing, dance, and eat together. It is a time to celebrate and show pride in their culture. Powwows can last from one afternoon to several days. The Indians dress in native costumes and dance ancient dances to the beating of drums.

Artists sell their arts and crafts. You might be able to buy some real Native American food cooked on an open fire. Native Americans go to powwows to be with each other, share ideas, and just have fun! Most powwows are also open to people who are not Indian. It's a great place to learn about Native American culture!

If you went to a powwow this weekend, what do you think you would see? What do you think might NOT be there? Circle the objects you think you would see at a powwow. Put an X through those you probably won't see.

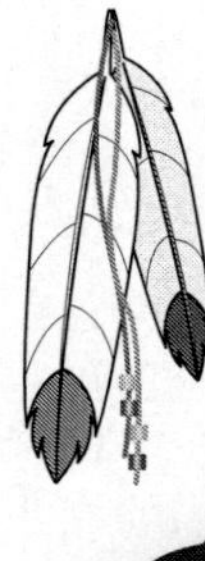

Answer Key: Circled objects are: beads, moccasins, open fire, drums, feathers, baskets, kids, food, drums, horse.

Make an Indian Weaving!

Many Native Americans used weaving to create useful things like sashes (belts), bags, mats, and blankets. They used animal hair to make yarn, and dyed the yarn with natural dyes from fruits and other plants. They also used some plant fibers, like cotton, to make weaving thread.

Weave a small Native American mat of your own. Use different colors of yarn to create a beautiful pattern in your weaving. Place a favorite object on the mat or hang it on your wall!

Prepare the "loom"

Cut a piece of cardboard 5 inches wide and 6 inches long. Along the two 5-inch sides (the "short" sides), have an adult cut slits 1/4 inch deep. These slits should be 1/2 inch apart from each other. So, on each short side you will have 9 slits.

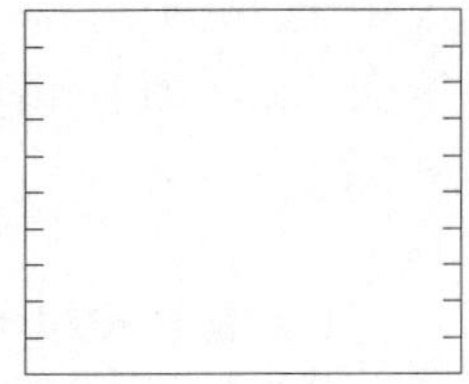

Directions:

1. Take a long piece of yarn and bring it from the back through the first slit (the one next to the edge of the cardboard.) The end of the yarn will hang down behind the cardboard.

2. Bring the yarn right across the front of the cardboard to the slit opposite the one your yarn came through.

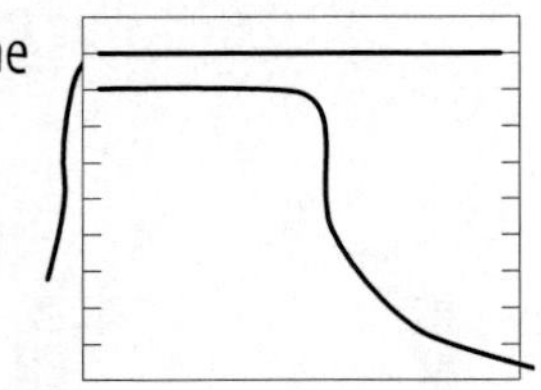

3. Now bring the yarn under the back of the cardboard and then up again through the second slit.

4. Repeat #2 and #3, until you have 9 strands of yarn across the front of your cardboard!

5. Then cut the yarn and tie the two loose ends in the back of the cardboard.

6. Take another piece of yarn and start feeding it through the 9 strands, going over one, under the next over the next, etc. When you get to the end, pull the yarn behind the cardboard and around to the front, and begin again. This time, whatever strand you went over, go under. And whatever strand you went under, go over.

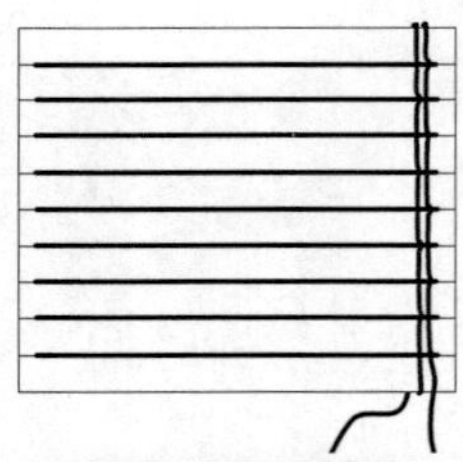

7. Repeat this pattern until the front of your cardboard in covered. Then cut the yarn in the back of the cardboard, and trim it to create a fringe for your mat!

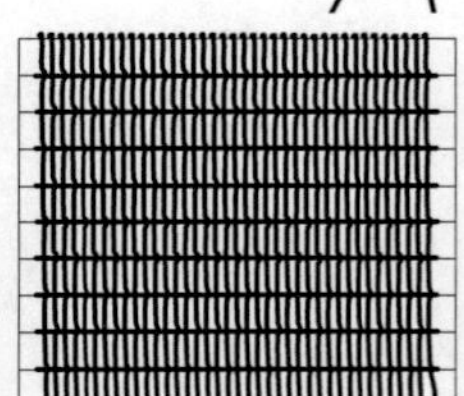

Tips:

- For a wild look, use variegated or different colored yarn!
- For a tighter mat, push the under/over strands up against the previous strands during weaving.
- To keep your mat from unravelling, tie neighboring fringe together up close to the mat.

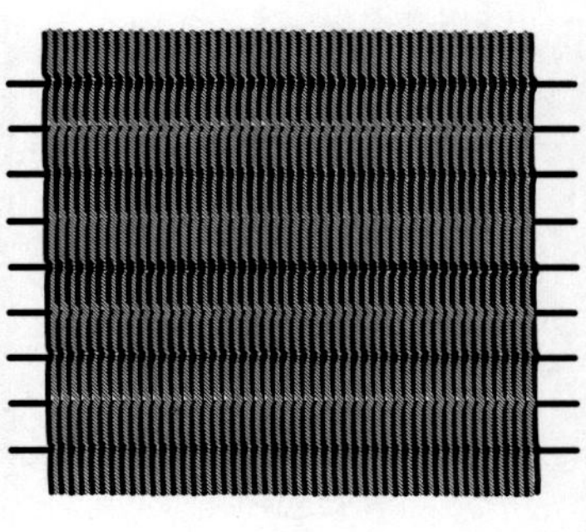

Finders Keepers?

Native Americans have many buried treasures. For hundreds of years, special objects would sometimes be buried with Native Americans, or maybe they would just be lost. Archeologists used to dig for interesting artifacts in old Native American gravesites. They would keep the Native American bones or the arrowheads, rattles, masks and other objects that they found. But this made the Native Americans feel like they were being robbed.

In 1990, the U.S. government passed a law that said that no one could look for or take these Native American objects anymore. And whoever had any already had to give them back to the people they belonged to. This is called repatriation

Help the archeologist return the artifact to a Native American.

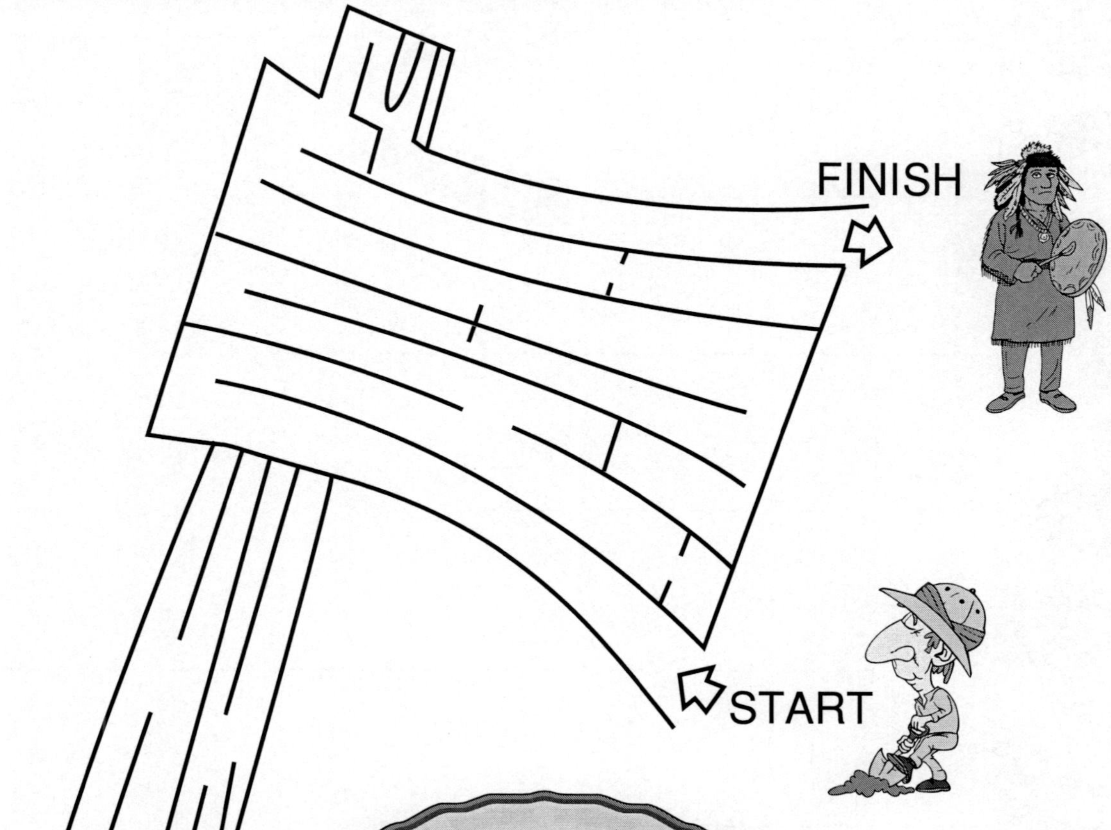

Fast Fact

An artifact is an object that was made by people a long time ago for some useful purpose.

Busy Hands!

Before modern times, Native Americans didn't have stores where they went to buy things. They made everything they needed.

What did Indians make with their own hands? Use the Word Bank and pictures to find out!

Word Bank

blanket	moccasins	arrows	pottery	canoe
mat	food	jewelry	pouch	box

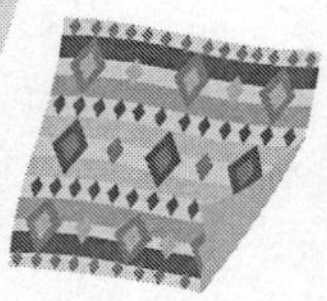
___ ___ ___

___ ___ ___ ___

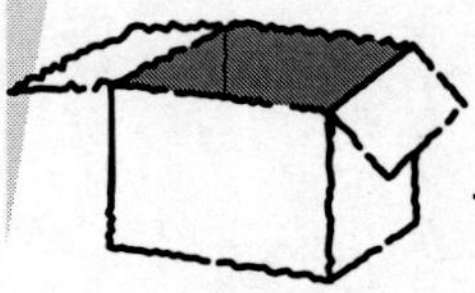
___ ___ ___

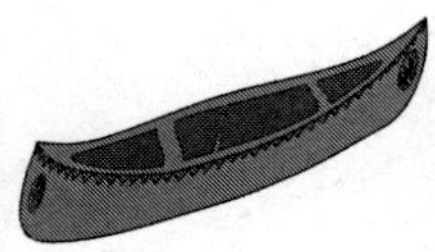
___ ___ ___ ___ ___

___ ___ ___ ___ ___ ___ ___

___ ___ ___ ___ ___

___ ___ ___ ___ ___ ___ ___ ___ ___ ___

___ ___ ___ ___ ___ ___

___ ___ ___ ___ ___ ___ ___

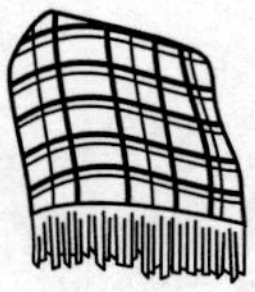
___ ___ ___ ___ ___ ___ ___

American Indians Today

Beginning with the first letter of each group of letters, cross out every other letter to discover some new words. You may not have heard of these before, but you can read all about them!

1. Many Indians live on these, but many more do not!

TRYELSDEBRNVJAOTPIPOWNASX

____

2. Many Indians have been poor for a long time because for many years the government took away their lands and their ability to make a living.

TPKOOVWEBRNTXYA

____

3. Many Indians have been studying hard at school and going to college in order to earn more money. Education helps the Indians make their lives better. These Native Americans are working to become:

TSJUMCBCFEYSMSOFPUVL

____

4. This is a big term that means Native Americans have worked hard to get the U.S. government to let them rule themselves. This means that they have their own laws and make their own decisions. They are like a separate country inside the U.S.! Now, try and see if you can get your parents to give you the same thing!

TSGENLBF ***JDGEETSEWRAMCIHNUAKTYIKOTNU***

__________________ ____

Fast Fact

What do Indians work as today?

- doctors
- nurses
- factory workers
- artists
- lawyers
- actors

The same kinds of jobs any American might work at!

Native Americans Move to the City!

Solve the code to discover the mystery words!

A	B	C	D	E	F	G	H	I	J	K	L	M
✷	❀	⌘	♣	➽	♥	❢	✫	✂	✆	☛	✈	✉
N	**O**	**P**	**Q**	**R**	**S**	**T**	**U**	**V**	**W**	**X**	**Y**	**Z**
✿	☆	✦	✡	✏	❥	☎	✒	✚	✖	✍	✠	✓

1. During the 1950s and 1960s, the American government paid Indians to leave their homes on reservations and move to cities to get jobs. If cities are sometimes called urban areas, then these brave Indians were called:

___ ___ ___ ___ ___   ___ ___ ___ ___ ___ ___ ___
✒ ✏ ❀ ✷ ✿   ✂ ✿ ♣ ✂ ✷ ✿ ❥

2. Many Indians chose to stay on their reservations and not move to the city. They thought that if they moved to the city, they would lose the way of life that their parents and ancestors had taught. These Indians called themselves:

___ ___ ___ ___ ___ ___ ___ ___ ___ ___ ___   ___ ___ ___ ___ ___ ___ ___
✏ ➽ ❥ ➽ ✏ ✚ ✷ ☎ ✂ ☆ ✿   ✂ ✿ ♣ ✂ ✷ ✿ ❥

3. Native Americans who moved to cities lived close to each other. They tried to keep their way of life as much as possible. They did not want to forget their religion, native art, or music. They did not want to lose their:

___ ___ ___ ___ ___ ___ ___
⌘ ✒ ✈ ☎ ✒ ✏ ➽

4. Are you afraid of heights? Many people are. The Mohawk Indians are not! Many of them work hundreds of feet above the city to build steel frames for skyscrapers. People who do this work above the city are:

___ ___ ___ ___ ___   ___ ___ ___ ___ ___ ___ ___
❥ ☎ ➽ ➽ ✈   ✖ ☆ ✏ ☛ ➽ ✏ ❥

5. Today urban Indians and reservation Indians come together to celebrate their culture. They share ideas and stories. They dance and beat drums. They make and sell Indian jewelry. During these celebrations, Indians remember how much they have to be proud of! These big parties are called

___ ___ ___ ___ ___ ___ ___
✦ ☆ ✖ ✖ ☆ ✖ ❥